D0628037

TO:

FROM:

Happiness

COMPILED BY

EVELYN BEILENSON

PETER PAUPER PRESS, INC.
White Plains, New York

Designed by Margaret Rubiano

Copyright © 2009
Peter Pauper Press, Inc.
202 Mamaroneck Avenue
White Plains, NY 10601
All rights reserved
ISBN 978-1-59359-775-7
Printed in China
7 6 5 4 3 2 1

Visit us at www.peterpauper.com

Happiness

Introduction

This little book is not about how to *find* happiness, the pursuit of which keeps happiness in the future and apart from us. This book is about how to *be* happiness. Here are beacons for the inward journey that connects us to the source of joy and brings us home. We are alive, so we might as well enjoy the dance.

But what is happiness
except the simple
harmony between a man
and the life he leads?

ALBERT CAMUS

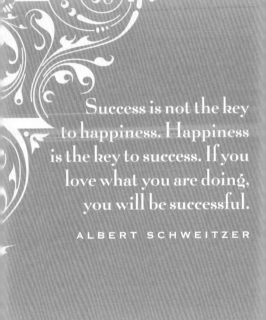

Success is not the key to happiness. Happiness is the key to success. If you love what you are doing, you will be successful.

ALBERT SCHWEITZER

The Grand essentials of happiness are: something to do, something to love, and something to hope for.

ALLAN K. CHALMERS

Happiness comes
when your work and
words are of benefit to
yourself and others.

BUDDHA

Happiness radiates like the fragrance from a flower, and draws all good things toward you. Allow your love to nourish yourself as well as others. Do not strain after the needs of life. It is sufficient to be quietly alert and aware of them. In this way life proceeds more naturally and effortlessly. Life is here to Enjoy!

MAHARISHI MAHESH YOGI

The basic thing is that everyone wants happiness, no one wants suffering. And happiness mainly comes from our own attitude, rather than from external factors. If your own mental attitude is correct, even if you remain in a hostile atmosphere, you feel happy.

THE DALAI LAMA

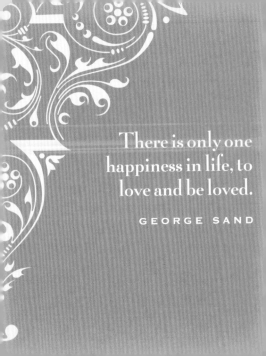

There is only one happiness in life, to love and be loved.

GEORGE SAND

The greatest part of
our happiness depends on
our dispositions, not
our circumstances.

MARTHA WASHINGTON

Happiness cannot come from without. It must come from within. It is not what we see and touch or that which others do for us which makes us happy; it is that which we think and feel and do, first for the other fellow and then for ourselves.

HELEN KELLER

Sometimes your joy is the source of your smile, but sometimes your smile can be the source of your joy.

THICH NHAT HANH

The happiest moments
of my life have been
the few which I have
passed at home in the
bosom of my family.

THOMAS JEFFERSON

When I meet people from other cultures I know that they too want happiness and do not want suffering; this allows me to see them as brothers and sisters.

CHARLES SCHULZ

The Constitution only guarantees the American people the right to pursue happiness. You have to catch it yourself.

BENJAMIN FRANKLIN

Nobody really cares if you're miserable, so you might as well be happy.

CYNTHIA NELMS

Happiness is when
what you think, what
you say, and what you
do are in harmony.

MOHANDAS K. GANDHI

Happiness is like a butterfly which, when pursued, is always beyond our grasp, but, if you will sit down quietly, may alight upon you.

NATHANIEL HAWTHORNE

If the sight of the blue skies fills you with joy, if a blade of grass springing up in the fields has power to move you, if the simple things in nature have a message you understand, Rejoice, for your soul is alive.

ELEANORA DUSE

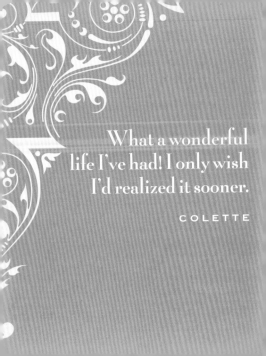

What a wonderful
life I've had! I only wish
I'd realized it sooner.

COLETTE

The best vitamin to
be a happy person is B1.

AUTHOR UNKNOWN

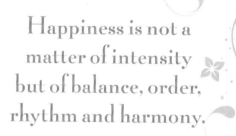

Happiness is not a
matter of intensity
but of balance, order,
rhythm and harmony.

THOMAS MERTON

Happiness is
a function of
accepting what is.

WERNER ERHARD

If you observe a really happy man you will find him building a boat, writing a symphony, educating his son, growing double dahlias in his garden, or looking for dinosaur eggs in the Gobi desert. He will not be searching for happiness as if it were a collar button that has rolled under the radiator. He will not be striving for it as a goal in itself. He will have become aware that he is happy in the course of living life twenty-four crowded hours of the day.

W. BERAN WOLFE

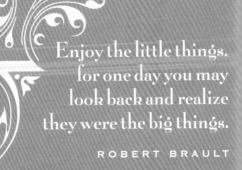

Enjoy the little things,
for one day you may
look back and realize
they were the big things.

ROBERT BRAULT

If you ever find happiness
by hunting for it, you will
find it, as the old woman
did her lost spectacles,
safe on her own nose
all the time.

JOSH BILLINGS

We are shaped by
our thoughts; we become
what we think. When
the mind is pure, joy
follows like a shadow
that never leaves.

BUDDHA

People take different roads seeking fulfillment and happiness. Just because they're not on your road doesn't mean they've gotten lost.

H. JACKSON BROWN, JR.

What we're looking for is happiness, and in all our searching who do we forget? Ourselves. Whatever the equation is that you have created, please include yourself in it, because without you, without your heart, without peace in your life, there can never be peace in the world.

PREM RAWAT

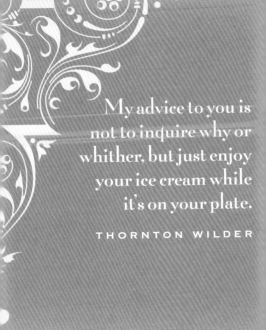

My advice to you is
not to inquire why or
whither, but just enjoy
your ice cream while
it's on your plate.

THORNTON WILDER

Happiness is not a
goal; it is a by-product.

ELEANOR ROOSEVELT

Jumping for
joy is good exercise.

AUTHOR UNKNOWN

I would maintain that
thanks are the highest
form of thought; and that
gratitude is happiness
doubled by wonder.

G.K. CHESTERTON

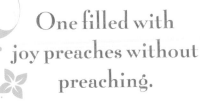

One filled with
joy preaches without
preaching.

MOTHER TERESA

One of my happiest moments of inspiration came to me many years ago as I lay on the grass, looking up into the leaves and branches of a big old tree in California. I remember feeling very much a part of everything and everyone.

JIM HENSON

Like swimming, riding, writing or playing golf, happiness can be learned.

DR. BORIS SOKOLOFF

Accept the pain, cherish the joys, resolve the regrets; then can come the best of benedictions— "If I had my life to live over, I'd do it all the same."

JOAN McINTOSH

For attractive lips, speak words of kindness. For lovely eyes, seek out the good in people. For a slim figure, share your food with the hungry. For beautiful hair, let a child run his or her fingers through it once a day.

AUDREY HEPBURN

The bird of paradise
alights only on the hand
that does not grasp.

JOHN BERRY

Life is not always
what one wants it to be,
but to make the best of
it as it is, is the only way
of being happy.

JENNIE JEROME CHURCHILL

One of the most responsible things you can do as an adult is to become more of a child.

DR. WAYNE W. DYER

I have learned to seek
my happiness by limiting
my desires, rather than
in attempting to
satisfy them.

JOHN STUART MILL

I am happy and content
because I think I am.

ALAIN-RENÉ LESAGE

The first recipe for
happiness is: Avoid
too lengthy meditations
on the past.

ANDRÉ MAUROIS

Happiness always looks small while you hold it in your hands, but let it go, and you learn at once how big and precious it is.

MAXIM GORKY

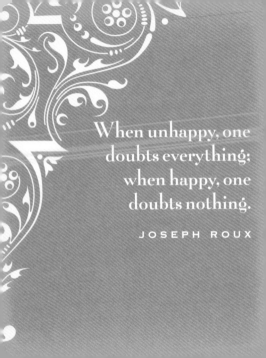

When unhappy, one
doubts everything;
when happy, one
doubts nothing.

JOSEPH ROUX

Perfect happiness is
the absence of striving
for happiness.

CHUANG-TZU

Happiness is the only sanction of life; where happiness fails, existence becomes a mad lamentable experiment.

GEORGE SANTAYANA

Who is rich?
He who rejoices
in his portion.

I have had more than half a century of such happiness. A great deal of worry and sorrow, too, but never a worry or a sorrow that was not offset by a purple iris, a lark, a bluebird, or a dewy morning glory.

MARY McLEOD BETHUNE

Happiness . . . leads none of us by the same route.

CHARLES CALEB COLTON

There is no cosmetic for beauty like happiness.

LADY MARGUERITE
BLESSINGTON

Make us happy
and you make us good.

ROBERT BROWNING

Happiness makes
up in height for what
it lacks in length.

ROBERT FROST

Weeping may endure
for a night, but joy
cometh in the morning.

PSALMS 30:5

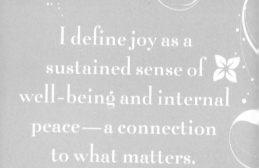

I define joy as a
sustained sense of
well-being and internal
peace—a connection
to what matters.

OPRAH WINFREY

Let your life lightly
dance on the edges of Time
like dew on the tip of a leaf.

RABINDRANATH TAGORE

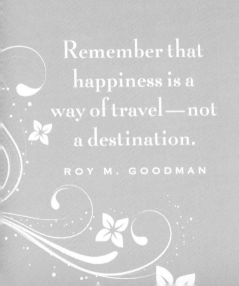

Remember that
happiness is a
way of travel—not
a destination.

ROY M. GOODMAN

People say that what we're seeking is a meaning for life. I don't think that's what we're really seeking. I think that what we're seeking is an experience of being alive, so that we actually feel the rapture of being alive.

JOSEPH CAMPBELL

Never lose the childlike wonder. It's just too important. It's what drives us.

RANDY PAUSCH

When you do
things from your soul,
you feel a river moving
in you, a joy.

RUMI

Even a happy life
cannot be without a
measure of darkness,
and the word happy
would lose its meaning
if it were not balanced
by sadness.

CARL JUNG

All I can say about life is,
Oh God, enjoy it!

BOB NEWHART

Happiness: a good bank
account, a good cook and
a good digestion.

JEAN JACQUES ROUSSEAU

Happiness is
an inside job.

WILLIAM ARTHUR WARD

Happiness is that
state of consciousness
which proceeds from
the achievement of
one's values.

AYN RAND

Happiness cannot be traveled to, owned, earned, worn or consumed. Happiness is the spiritual experience of living every minute with love, grace and gratitude.

DENIS WAITLEY

Happiness often sneaks in
through a door you didn't
know you left open.

JOHN BARRYMORE

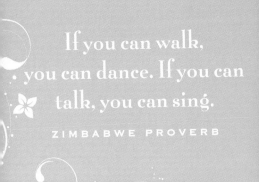

If you can walk,
you can dance. If you can
talk, you can sing.

ZIMBABWE PROVERB

The best years of your life are the ones in which you decide your problems are your own. You do not blame them on your mother, the ecology, or the president. You realize that you control your own destiny.

ALBERT ELLIS

It isn't what you have,
or who you are, or where
you are, or what you are
doing that makes you
happy or unhappy. It is
what you think about.

DALE CARNEGIE

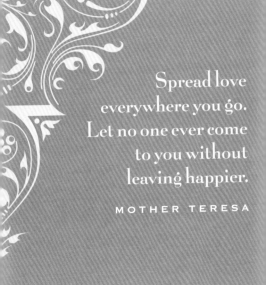

Spread love
everywhere you go.
Let no one ever come
to you without
leaving happier.

MOTHER TERESA

Be happy for this moment.
This moment is your life.

OMAR KHAYYAM

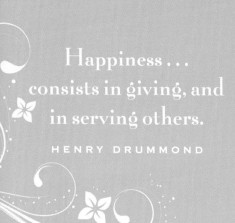

Happiness . . .
consists in giving, and
in serving others.

HENRY DRUMMOND

All happiness
depends on a
leisurely breakfast.

JOHN GUNTHER

Isn't precisely
happiness what we all
want, without exception?

SAINT AUGUSTINE

Be glad of life because
it gives you the chance
to love and to work and
to play and to look up
at the stars.

HENRY VAN DYKE

Family life is the
source of the greatest
human happiness.

ROBERT J. HAVIGHURST

Talk happiness. The world is sad enough without your woe. No path is wholly rough.

ELLA WHEELER WILCOX

The secret to happiness
is happiness itself. Wherever
we are, any time, we have
the capacity to enjoy the
sunshine, the presence of
each other, and the wonder
of our breathing.

THICH NHAT HANH

There is no cure for
birth and death save to
enjoy the interval.

GEORGE SANTAYANA

Maybe we should develop a Crayola bomb as our next secret weapon. A happiness weapon. A beauty bomb. And every time a crisis developed, we would launch one. It would explode high in the air—explode softly—and send thousands, millions, of little parachutes into the air. Floating down to earth—boxes of Crayolas.

ROBERT FULGHUM

If you follow your bliss, doors will open for you that wouldn't have opened for anyone else.

JOSEPH CAMPBELL